Springboard for Overlord

Hampshire and the D-Day Landings

ANTHONY KEMP

Down Memory Lane I linger long,
Till evening shadows fall,
To dream of golden days bygone,
And radiant hours recall.

MILESTONE PUBLICATIONS

Phototypesetting by Inforum Ltd, Portsmouth
Printed by Conifer Press, Fareham.

Published by Milestone Publications
The Publishing and Bookselling Division
of Goss & Crested China Limited
62 Murray Road Horndean Hants PO8 9JL

First impression 1984

British Library Cataloguing in Publication Data

Kemp, Anthony
    Springboard for Overlord.—(Down memory lane; 16)
    1. World War, 1939–1945—England—Hampshire
    2. Hampshire—History, Military
    I. Title   II. Series
    940.54′21   D760.8.H2

ISBN 0–903852–42–X

FOREWORD

In the Spring of 1944 I was five. I had been evacuated from London and exchanged life in the cellar of our suburban house for the Hampshire countryside. As a wartime child, my earliest memories were conditioned by air-raid sirens, gas masks and the sight of uniforms. I knew that there was a war but at that stage in my life, I could not conceive any other situation – it was just something that was accepted.

On arrival in Liphook I discovered a new world of fields, farm animals and peace. I well remember the weekly walk to collect my free bottle of welfare orange juice and the arrival of huge red apples – the gift of the Canadian people to the children of Britain. Also there was the weekly expedition to the bicycle shop to have the accumulator for the radio charged. That radio in its monumental walnut cabinet was the grown-ups' link with the outside world. Everyone gathered around it to listen to the 'news' and my small ears associated the wireless with the opening bars of Beethoven's 5th Symphony and Lillibulero – that fine old marching tune that Marlborough's men sang on the long road to Blenheim.

Soon however, our rural peace was shattered by an invasion – it must have been towards the end of April 1944. Military vehicles had been a familiar sight on the A3 through the village and the vast Bordon camp was only down the road. But from then on, that same road was choked with new traffic for months on end. The orchard at the end of our garden became a camp which housed groups of soldiers who came for a day or two and then moved on. Like soldiers the world over, these strangers – British, Canadians and others speaking unknown languages, welcomed the small boy who stood there shyly watching their activi-

ties. My collection of cap badges grew, as did my knowledge of various types of vehicle. I tried on their hats and I sampled their cooking. I admired the red-capped military policemen who directed the traffic and learnt to salute officers. Too young to be at school, those Spring days are etched into my memory. The grown-ups told me that the soldiers were going to somewhere a long way away over the sea and were going to win the war – which I did not understand except that this was going to be a good thing.

As I write this it seems to me that I can recall a sense of expectancy – but perhaps my memory is playing tricks. One thing, however, is crystal clear. One morning I stood in the garden with an adult as masses of aircraft flew over heading south. I asked why two aeroplanes were tied together and was told that they were gliders. What I had seen were the gliders heading for Normandy to back up the airborne landings early on the morning of 6 June.

After a while, the traffic through the village grew thinner and there was talk of peace. I went back to London, celebrated VE Day and was taken to see the victory parade. For me, the war was over.

As a writer and historian, I am often asked – 'Why do we celebrate such anniversaries as D-Day or some such other battle? Is it not immoral to be glorifying war?' The short answer is that there is little glory to be had for anyone in war, but as a form of human activity it has been with us for a long time and will not simply disappear as a result of pious wishes expressed by campaigners for 'peace'. For most of those who took part in it, the Second World War (or any other war for that matter) was the

The scene on the beach at Bernières-sur-Mer on D-Day with pioneers making roadways for heavy vehicles. Armoured bulldozer in the right foreground.

The site of S.1 Hard today with Berth 101 to the left.   *A. Kemp collection*

single most important event in their lives – whether they were in the armed forces or caught up in events as civilians. The war as a whole was to profoundly alter the society in which we live today, and was fought for a just cause. It is therefore worth remembering the events of the war and to spare a thought for those who did not return.

The aim of this little book is not to glorify, but to set out some of the background to the important role played by the South Hampshire area in Operation Overlord – the aim of which was to liberate Europe from vicious oppression. As a direct result, we are now a part of that Europe which has managed ever since to live at peace – for the first time in centuries.

Remains of the Mulberry Harbour at Arromanches. A 'slug' pontoon used to support sections of 'Whale' roadway.

A. Kemp collection

6

TOTAL WAR

War was no stranger to the Solent area. During the Middle Ages, Southampton was perhaps the premier port of England with important trading links to Europe, as well as being a favourite place of embarkation for overseas military expeditions. The town was sacked by the French in 1337 at the start of the 100 Years War, but after that, the fortifications were considerably strengthened, together with the royal castle. In 1346, Edward III assembled his army at Southampton and sailed forth on the campaign that was to culminate in the victory at Crecy. Another army embarked for France in 1415 under the command of Henry V at the start of the expedition leading to triumph at Agincourt.

After that, Southampton as a port declined in importance, and Henry VII chose Portsmouth as the site for the first dry-dock to be built in the country, thus paving the way for development of Britain's chief naval base – a function that still prevails today. From Portsmouth and the sheltered anchorage of Spithead, the British Navy dominated the Channel and kept potential enemies away from our coasts. If Portsmouth was the home of the Navy, Southampton during the 19th century enjoyed a rebirth as a port. In 1840 the railway line to London started operating and at the same time, new docks were being built. Most of the troops shipped out to the Crimea left from there, and the sad human wreckage of that war was delivered back to the new military hospital founded at Netley.

It was the same story during the Boer War and the First World War, when the docks of Southampton fed the front line with troops and stores, while the naval base at Portsmouth ensured the freedom of the seas.

As the clouds of war gathered over Europe once again, the population was issued with gas masks, plans to evacuate children from the towns were made and air raid shelters were constructed. In March 1937, watched by only a few people at Eastleigh Aerodrome, the prototype Spitfire flew for the first time.

The summer of 1939 is remembered by many for the beautiful weather, and the beaches of the South were crowded with holidaymakers – for the last time for six fateful years. As the crisis deepened, the fleet slipped out of Portsmouth to take up its war stations, and on 30 August, the *Queen Mary* left Southampton for America. Shortly afterwards, the troops of the British Expeditionary Force embarked as so often in the past for France, little dreaming that in less than a year they would be returning. In May and June 1940 the troops returned mingling with the hordes of refugees. The harbours in the Solent area were soon crowded with foreign fishing boats, yachts and coasting steamers. The siege of Britain was about to begin.

Britain in that summer of 1940 was already a nation totally immersed in war, with black-out restrictions, rationing and shortages. Portsmouth, as a military installation was reasonably well protected with anti-aircraft weapons, but Southampton was virtually defenceless. It was obvious that the Supermarine works and the port installations would be a prime target for air raids, and a civilian infrastructure of Auxiliary Fire Service and Air Raid Precautions personnel had been created. Almost everyone had some form of extra duty occasioned by the war. In Portsmouth it was the same story, with ARP main control located in Hewitt Road.

Along the beaches, scaffolding poles were bolted together to form an anti-invasion fence and pill-boxes were constructed at

The New Docks at Southampton in peacetime with the Solent Flour Mills in the background. Hard S.1 was constructed at Berth 101 for loading landing craft. Southampton City Museums, Hallett Jerrard Collection

Bomb damage to a warehouse in Southampton Docks.
• *Southampton City Museums, Hallett Jerrard Collection*

strategic sites. Windows were criss-crossed with tape and entrances to many buildings were blocked with sandbag anti-blast walls. Many of the children had already departed and on 4 July, Hampshire beaches were closed to the public during daylight. On 8 July, the south of Hampshire was declared a restricted area and the entry of visitors was prohibited.

Throughout the autumn and winter, German bombers cruised overhead. Both Portsmouth and Southampton together with the surrounding suburbs suffered immense damage, the centres of both cities being more or less obliterated. Thousands were made homeless, but somehow the authorities managed to cope, helped by a whole army of volunteers. In spite of the damage, life continued and so did industry. In Portsmouth, the Dockyard worked around the clock building and repairing warships, sup-plying and arming them and sending them back to sea. In South-ampton, after the main Supermarine works was blitzed, aircraft production was spread all over the place in garages, factories and small workshops. Other aircraft were built at the Airspeed works at Portsmouth and the Folland factory at Hamble. Thorney-croft's yard at Woolston turned out destroyers and the repair works of Harland and Wolff in the docks was never idle. Even after the main blitz was over, tension never entirely diminished, as there were regular tip and run raids which tested the mettle of the defences. It was against this background of constant toil for the common war effort, that the story of D-Day was to unfold.

OVERLORD

There is no disputing the fact that Operation Overlord, the invasion of occupied Europe by Allied forces on 6 June 1944 was the greatest amphibious operation every mounted in the history of war – and that it was a victory. D-Day, the actual invasion date in military jargon, however, was only the start of a long and arduous campaign which was not to end until Germany finally collapsed in the Spring of the following year. To understand events as they impinged on our local region, it is necessary first to survey the broader issues of how the plan was conceived and then carried out.

In those far off grim days in June 1940 with our forces having been booted unceremoniously from the Continent and our fight for survival in the air about to begin, Winston Churchill broadcast to the defeated French –

'Good night then, sleep to gather strength for the morning, for the morning will come, brightly will it shine on the brave and cool, kindly on all who suffer for the cause – Vive la France'.

At that time, other than a few pin-prick raids carried out by the new shock troops known as Commandos, there was nothing that Britain could do to dislodge the Germans from France, and it was not until December 1941 when America entered the war, that the balance began to tilt in our favour.

Although Churchill was often in favour of hare-brained schemes of invasion through Norway, Greece and the Balkan countries, it was obvious to serious military planners that the only way to defeat Germany was by the shortest route – across the Channel, into France and then to head for the Rhine. During the early part of 1942, the Americans were full of enthusiasm for cross-Channel operations in that Summer, and the Russians were pleading for a full-blown invasion to relieve some of the pressure on their beleaguered forces. Sober British wisdom managed to prevail, but a major raid was planned to capture the port of Dieppe, described at the time as a 'reconnaissance in force'. This took place in August 1942 and was a total disaster. Half the force embarked, mostly Canadians, were either killed or captured. The raid was badly planned, the troops were poorly equipped and insufficiently trained. The German propaganda made a meal of the defeat and issued pictures of wrecked equipment and dead bodies littered on the shingle.

Although it was no consolation to those who died there, a number of important lessons were learnt at Dieppe. Firstly, a frontal attack on a defended port was useless unless it was first subjected to a massive bombardment – which in turn would destroy those very harbour facilities which the attack had been designed to capture in the first place. Secondly, the importance of massive naval fire support during the assault phase – at Dieppe only a few lightly gunned destroyers were available. Although Montgomery was later to remark that those lessons could have been learnt more cheaply without the sacrifice of a fine Canadian division, they were taken to heart and applied two years afterwards on the beaches of Normandy.

The genesis of Overlord is to be found in the deliberations of the Allied leaders at Casablanca in January 1943. There, it was decided that a cross-Channel operation would not be possible that year, but that a planning organisation should be set up with an invasion in the Summer of 1944 as a target. It was further agreed that a British officer would head this body, with the title of Chief of Staff to the Supreme Allied Commander (designate), hence the name by which it is generally known – COSSAC. The person appointed was Lieutenant-General F.E. Morgan, but it was not until the end of April that he received his instructions from the Combined Chiefs of Staff.

In May, at the Allied summit held in Washington (Trident), a target date of 1 May 1944 was set and General Morgan was given some idea of the forces which would be made available. He and his planners were expected to come up with an outline plan by 1 August.

The COSSAC staff had naturally inherited much expertise that had been collected by Combined Operations and other groups who had been considering various means of landing on the Continent. They soon narrowed their options down to two areas – the Pas de Calais and the Caen area of the Normandy coast. The former would have seemingly been the more favourable – within sight of the French coast, within range for maximum fighter cover and offering the shortest route to Germany. Because it was so obvious, however, it had naturally been more heavily fortified by the Germans, and the harbours on the Kent coast were too small to accomodate a large assault force. On the other hand, the beaches in Normandy were ideal for landing troops, were still within range of fighter aircraft operating from Britain and were less strongly fortified. In addition, Cherbourg and the ports in Brittany would become available once a lodgement had been secured.

General Morgan had been allotted limited forces on paper and he envisaged a landing on a three division front with airborne and Commando support. This outline was approved in August at the 'Quadrant' conference in Quebec, and Morgan was ordered to start planning in detail. His problem was that he was operating in a vacuum as Chief of Staff to a still unappointed Supreme Commander – who might well have ideas of his own, and would

probably be an American.

Morgan's plan was largely determined by factors outside his control, namely the number of landing craft that could be made available to lift his assault force. Both the Mediterranean and the Pacific theatres were clamouring for landing craft of different types and building yards in this country and America were working at full capacity. Furthermore, lurking in the background was the plan for a simultaneous landing in the South of France – to be known as Anvil – which in turn would also require landing craft.

During November and early December 1943, the next series of Allied summit conferences were held at Cairo and Teheran. There, it was agreed that Overlord would go ahead in early May and that the Supreme Commander would be General Dwight D Eisenhower, who would be transferred from the Mediterranean. His orders were – 'You will enter the continent of Europe and, in conjunction with other United Nations, undertake operations aimed at the heart of Germany and the destruction of her armed forces'.

Slightly earlier, in October, Admiral Sir Bertram Ramsay had been appointed as Naval head of Overlord, and in November, Air Marshal Sir Trafford Leigh-Mallory received instructions which defined his command of the tactical air forces. This left the question of who would command the ground forces still open. The British and Canadian forces assembled in England for Overlord were known as 21st Army Group, commanded by General Paget, whose headquarters were in St. Paul's School in London. In the general shift around of commands, Paget was sent to take over in the Middle East, and General Bernard Law Montgomery was transferred from Italy to take command of 21st Army Group. This meant that he would be the overall commander of ground troops – British and American – for the assault phase and until the Americans built up enough forces to form their own army group. The choice of Montgomery was a popular one in

General Montgomery, commander of 21st Army Group visiting Portsmouth in January 1944.

England, as the victor of Alamein was already a familiar figure on the newsreels, the famous black beret with two badges at a jaunty angle. Eisenhower, however, would have preferred Alexander, with whom he had worked well in North Africa. In the abrasive personality of Montgomery were sown the seeds of future discord, but without doubt, he was the most competent soldier available, either British or American.

At the turn of the year, on his way back to England, he stopped off in Morocco to visit Winston Churchill who was convalescing there from a bout of pneumonia. The Prime Minister showed him the COSSAC plan, and Monty instantly realised that it was envisaged on a far too narrow front. On arrival in London, he worked out a new proposal which called for an assault by five divisions instead of three, and a widening of the front to include the eastern part of the Cotentin Peninsula – to

ease the capture of Cherbourg. By the end of January, both Eisenhower and the Combined Chiefs of Staff had accepted the Montgomery plan, but were then faced with the problem of finding the necessary extra resources. Both the Air Force and the Navy submitted their lists, and the most grievous shortage was in respect of shipping, both for movement of supplies and troops. In the end, it was resolved to postpone Overlord until the end of May, and after much argument behind the scenes, to defer Anvil until such a time as landing craft could be transferred back to the Mediterranean.

The basic object of Overlord was to secure a bridgehead in France from which further operations could be mounted. The assault phase of the operation was code-named Neptune, which envisaged the landing of five divisions between the mouth of the River Orne and the neck of the Cotentin Peninsula. To seal off the battlefield, airborne troops would be dropped at either end in advance of the actual landings. The coast was divided into two sectors, British and American and subdivided into five actual beaches –

American First Army	Utah	4th Inf. Div.
	Omaha	1st Inf. Div.
British Second Army	Gold	50th Inf. Div.
	Juno	3rd Canadian Inf. Div.
	Sword	3rd Inf. Div.

To bombard the coast, land vehicles, troops and stores, sweep mines and secure the approaches, nearly 7,000 vessels were employed, from barges to battleships. Flying over this vast Armada were the fighters and bombers of the American and British air forces. Their task was to protect the convoys and neutralise the German defences along the coast. Before D-Day itself, total air superiority had to be established and enemy

Landing Ship Tank in the Solent.   Copyright 'The News', Portsmouth

Portsmouth, and Montgomery's Tactical Headquarters was set up in the grounds. On that day also, the main orders for the concentration of troops into the embarkation areas were issued. On 17 May the provisional date of 5 June was laid down with the option of postponement for two further days. After that, the tides would be unsuitable for a further two weeks and such a delay could well have spelled the end of the operation for that year. For the war-weary people of southern Hampshire, a new chapter in their lives was about to unfold, although naturally enough, they were not informed of the fact.

communications cut, to hinder reinforcements being brought into the battle area.

Although ports between Milford Haven and the Thames Estuary were earmarked for the shipping of Overlord forces, once the decision had been made to land in Normandy, it was obvious geographically that the main concentration would have to be centred on the Solent. As we shall see in the next chapter, the area was already home to a considerable number of Combined Operations organisations and other outfits spawned by COSSAC. By the time Eisenhower and Montgomery took over, most of the background preparation had been completed. Intelligence had been gathered, logistics systems laid down, routes to the embarkation points reconnoitred, shipping assembled and equipment stockpiled.

On 26 April 1944, the staff of the Naval Commander, Admiral Ramsey, moved into Southwick House just to the north of

Canadian infantry on manoeuvre defending the Hilsea Lines.

Copyright 'The News', Portsmouth

12

PRELUDE TO OVERLORD

Overlord did not just happen, as we have seen in the previous chapter. It was the product of a number of high level decisions and a lengthy period of planning. To achieve success, a number of major problems had to be solved and the infrastructure of amphibious warfare had to exist. In October 1941, the then Captain Lord Louis Mountbatten had been appointed to succeed Sir Roger Keyes as head of Combined Operations, and the following April he was accorded equal status with the Chiefs-of-Staff of the other arms of the forces. Described by one author as 'brilliant but flighty', he and Churchill were equally determined to carry the war into the enemy's camp.

Combined Operations

Early in 1942, a whole network of Combined Operations units began to appear in the Solent area. Headquarters was set up deep in the bowels of the Victorian Fort Southwick on Portsdown Hill, and the Landing Craft Base HQ was HMS *Porcupine*. The latter was two thirds of a destroyer which had been salvaged and brought back from the Mediterranean. In charge of all this activity was the Commodore Combined Operations Bases, Portsmouth Command.

HMS *Manatee*, *Vectis* and *Medina* were respectively located at Yarmouth, Cowes and Ryde, the latter in the Puckpool Holiday Camp. They were all landing craft bases, and HMS *Medina* ultimately became responsible for the training of Thames bargees who together with their barges were requisitioned for Overlord.

HMS *Squid* was a shore base at Elmfield Court in Millbrook, with a sub unit at Hythe, and HMS *Mastodon* was at Exbury, responsible for a flotilla of tank landing craft (LCT's).

The Nautical College at Warsash became HMS *Tormentor* and the whole of the Hamble River facilities became devoted to the maintenance of landing craft. Also at Warsash was the School of Raiding, home of the Small Scale Raiding Force (SSRF) which was established in February 1942. Their preferred type of craft was the CNI Dory, which had been developed by the yacht builders, Camper and Nicholsons.

Almost the whole of Hayling Island became occupied by various offshoots of Combined Operations. HMS *Northney* was a training unit for landing craft personnel, and HMS *Dragonfly* – which consisted of a number of bathing huts on the shore of Langstone Harbour, was a maintenance base. In the summer of 1942, the Hayling Island Sailing Club was taken over by the Combined Operations Pilotage Parties (COPP), whose activities will be detailed later.

An official total of 61 raids were carried out against the occupied coastline of Europe between Holland and the Spanish border, many of which were planned to gain information about the German defences – the so-called Atlantic Wall – and to let the Germans know that we were still in the war. During the summer of 1942, Forfar Force was formed from men of 12 Commando as a direct ancestor of today's Royal Marines. Special Boat Squadron (SBS), and they trained in cliff climbing techniques at Freshwater Bay. Sallying forth from their base at Warsash, they carried out a number of daring raids on the French coast until their disbandment in November 1943. The responsibility for raiding then devolved upon a new unit known as Layforce II, many of whose men were French-speaking refugees from 10 (Inter-Allied) Commando. One of the missions entrusted to Layforce was to concentrate their efforts in the Pas de Calais area as part

Canadian troops practising a beach assault during training.

Public archives of Canada

of the general pre-Overlord deception plans.

Another small unit based in the Solent area was the Royal Marine Boom Patrol Detachment housed at Eastney Barracks – the original Cockleshell Heroes. Ostensibly their job was to patrol the net boom that stretched between the Southsea shore and the Isle of Wight via the Victorian sea forts, dropping small charges into the water to discourage German swimmers. In December 1942, under the command of Major 'Blondie' Haslar they carried out the famous raid on shipping in Bordeux harbour, from which only two of the ten men returned – Haslar and Corporal Sparks.

Specialist Armoured Vehicles

One of the small group of British officers who pioneered the use of tanks between the wars was Major-General Percy Hobart, known generally as 'Hobo', who incidentally was Montgomery's brother-in-law. Hobart was forced to retire from the army on account of his supposed 'unorthodox' views and in 1940 was serving as a corporal in the Home Guard. Rescued from oblivion by direct order of Churchill, he was put in charge of the development of armoured vehicles designed to perform specialist tasks. He set up his small organisation at Bovington in Dorset, the home of the Royal Tank Regiment, and from his workshops there emerged a whole series of armoured vehicles that were to play a decisive role on D-Day and in the campaign in north-west Europe. Many of these vehicles were given animal names as a cover, hence the nick name of Hobart's Menagerie.

The Crab or flail tank was a device for clearing minefields and barbed wire, consisting of a rotating drum on the front of a conventional tank. This had lengths of chain attached which literally flailed or beat a path through the mines. The Crocodile was a Churchill tank chassis, fitted with a flame-thrower, a weapon much feared by the Germans. The fuel was towed be-

hidn the tank in a specially designed armoured trailer.

One of the lessons learnt at Dieppe was the difficulty for tanks of crossing obstacles such as sea walls and anti-tank ditches. To cope with this, Hobart developed a number of bridge carrying-vehicles including the Arc. The Bobbin uncoiled a matting roadway from a huge drum to lay a path over soft sand and the fascine could drop a large bundle of branches into a crater or ditch. These vehicles were all versions of the Armoured Vehicle Royal Engineers (AVRE) which could also be used for firing a heavy explosive charge at concrete fortifications. Instead of the normal gun in the turret, a large spigot mortar was fitted. The projectile from this was known as the 'flying dustbin' owing to its size.

Other devices did not progress much further than initial tests, many of which were carried out on beaches in the South, including the 'Panjandrum'. This was like a large Catharine Wheel designed to crash through barbed wire, which when tested ran amok. Highly successful, however was the Sherman Duplex Drive (DD) tank. This was a truly swimmable tank which was kept afloat by collapsible canvas screens. The engine could drive either propellors or the tracks, and on D-Day, the DD tanks swam onto the beaches to support the initial infantry attack waves.

In early 1943, all these vehicles (other than the DD's) were formed into the 79th Armoured Division commanded by Hobart. The Americans proved sceptical and other than the DD, did not accept the help offered. On the British beaches, specialist armour was to prove invaluable and saved a considerable number of lives.

Pluto

These initials literally stood for Pipe Line Under The Ocean, an idea which was born as far back as April 1942. At that time, Lord

Louis Mountbatten was considering the problems of fuel supplies to an army which had landed on the Continent, and asked officials at the Petroleum Department to come up with some ideas. During the following year a number of trials were undertaken and two systems were developed, both of which were in fact to be used after D-Day. The first was a flexible hollow cable known as Hais, which could be laid on the sea bed in the same manner as telephone cables. The other was called Hamel and consisted of lengths of 3″ diameter steel pipe which could be welded together and coiled onto 30 foot diameter drums. These were known as Conums and were disguised under the cover name HMS *Conundrum*. The first lengths of Hamel pipe were welded in Portsmouth Dockyard before a special factory set up at Tilbury was ready to start production.

In August 1943, a naval detachment took over the remains of the bombed out Supermarine factory at Woolston, which was christened HMS *Albatos*. It became the headquarters of the Senior Naval Officer, Force Pluto, who was Captain J. F. Hutchins RN. Shortly before D-Day, headquarters were transferred to 21 Upper Vicarage Road in Woolston. HMS *Albatos* served as a training base for those employed on the Pluto project and serviced the motley collection of vessels which had been commandeered.

Initial laying tests with Hamel pipe were carried out from a drum mounted in a converted Thames lighter, HMS *Persephone*, while the Conums were still being built. In April 1944, an eleven mile loop of Hamel was laid off Bournemouth from a Conum and petrol was successfully pumped through. In the meanwhile, both Hais and Hamel pipes were laid between Lepe Beach and Gurnard Point on the Isle of Wight, from whence fuel could be taken by land pipelines to the Sandown area. There, the Royal Engineers built two pumping stations, one at Sandown and the other at Shanklin, as the shore end of the pipes that were to cross the Channel.

Tests had shown that 70 miles of Hamel pipe could be wound onto a Conundrum, which needed two of the most powerful ocean going tugs to tow it, and that it could be unwound at a speed of up to seven knots.

Operation Pluto could not get underway until 12 August 1944, owing to the delay in capturing Cherbourg, but two Hais cables and two Hamel pipes were rapidly working to supply Allied forces in Normandy. Later, a further group of pipes was laid between Dungeness and Boulogne. In all, 172 million gallons of petrol were supplied through Pluto, which continued in operation until July 1945, pumping into a system of land pipelines reaching out well inside Germany itself. General Eisenhower later commented that Pluto was 'second only in daring to the artificial harbours projects'. For some while after the war, several Conundrums could be seen off Netley, although few who saw them had any real idea of their purpose.

Mulberry Harbours

As early as the First World War, Winston Churchill had suggested the use of concrete elements to form an artificial harbour, and he returned to the subject in May 1942 when Combined Operations were considering ways and means for a cross-Channel assault. In a memo. to Mountbatten he referred to piers for use on open beaches which 'must float up and down with the tide'. War Office planners turned their attention to the idea, but it was not until June 1943 that the scheme of providing complete harbours was seriously mooted. By then, the awful lesson of Dieppe had been absorbed – that it was impossible to capture a defended port – and the planners thought that it was unlikely that Cherbourg and the Brittany harbours would be free for use until D-Day + 40. The COSSAC staff came up with a requirement for two artificial harbours each the size of Dover which could be towed in sections across the Channel and be assembled

Specialist armour. Two examples of the type known as an AVRE. On the right is a spigot mortar (flying dustbin) and on the left, a fascine.

Public archives of Canada

Phoenix caisson nearing completion at Southampton. Beside it is another still under construction.

Southampton City Museums, Hallett Jerrard Collection

Rhino ferry units and Mulberry pierheads.

Southampton City Museums, Hallett Jerrard Collection

off the Normandy beaches. Typical of the speed at which planners worked during the war, the basic outline of the scheme was ready by the end of August and construction work started in September. The basic scheme was as follows. As soon as possible after the actual landings, lines of old ships (Corncobs) were to be sunk off each beach to form a breakwater or Gooseberry. These would provide a modicum of shelter for immediate unloading operations.

In the meanwhile, the first units of the artificial harbours would be on their way across the Channel, consisting of concrete caissons known as Phoenix's. Each of these was almost as big as a five storey block of flats, measuring 200 feet in length, 55 feet in width and 60 feet high. Their total weight was 6,000 tons each. The Phoenix Caissons would be joined onto the line of 'Corn-

cobs' to form an outer breakwater, and when flooded would sit firmly on the bottom of the sea. The next stage was then to construct floating roadways running out from the beach connected to steel pierheads known as Whales. These slid up and down on Spud legs standing on the bottom. One Mulberry was to be located near the British beaches at the small seaside resort of Arromanches, and the other, for the Americans at Omaha Beach.

To give just some idea of the scale of the operations, a total of some two million tons of pre-fabricated material had to be towed across the channel and assembled. Seventy four obsolete ships were used as Corncobs, and 213 Phoenix caissons were built. Ten miles of Whale roadway had to be built, as well as 93 Bombardons. These were huge floating pontoons designed to

Phoenix caisson under construction in Southampton Docks.

Southampton City Museums, Hallett Jerrard Collection

'Rhino' ferries in Southampton Water. In the background is Mulberry pierhead. Southampton City Museums, Hallett Jerrard Collection

Mulberry pierhead with spud legs in the raised position under tow off the Western Docks. Southampton City Museums, Hallett Jerrard Collection

form a further breakwater unit for deep draught ships to seaward of the Mulberries. Every available tug both in Britain and the United States was pressed into service to transport the mass of material.

Various parts of the country were involved in construction of Mulberry harbour units, but the main concentration was in the Solent area. As far as Portsmouth was concerned, Messrs John Laing, the contractors, set up a plant to manufacture sections of Whale roadway on Clarence Beach. Soon they outgrew their allotted space and requested permission to store completed lengths on Pier Road. After a certain amount of argument on the part of the Council, the Ministry of Supply simply closed the road to enable storage of 'certain devices being manufactured on Clarence Beach'.

Southampton Harbour, already bursting at the seams with

landing craft, became the main Mulberry centre in the country. As early as September 1943 No. 7 Dock was allocated for the construction of Bombardons, and No. 5 Dock for Phoenix's. The latter, 800 feet long, permitted the construction of three at a time, ultimately employing some 1,000 men on a two shift system. As the units were completed they were berthed in the docks until being towed to an area in the sea off Selsey, where they were sunk in the hope of avoiding detection from the air. In theory, when required, they would be pumped out and rise to the surface. In fact, considerable difficulties were encountered just prior to D-Day, as many of the Phoenix's refused to surface from the sea bed. In his diary for 25 May 1944, General Alan Brooke noted – '. . . hurried lunch and dash to Portsmouth where motor launch took me to vicinity of Isle of Wight to see the "Whales" new piers for the invasion. A wonderful sight.

From there to Selsey Bill to see the "Phoenixes", the large concrete caissons for the breakwaters for the artificial harbours. They had been towed to this spot and then sunk in rows, so that they stuck out of the water like a row of houses.'

In the New Docks area, Royal Engineers were busy constructing Rhino's, which were large floating rafts propelled by outboard motors, designed to carry vehicles from LST's to the beach. The King George V Graving Dock was fully occupied with the assembly of Bombardons.

Sections of Whale roadway were built all over the place, and besides Portsmouth, the Military Port at Marchwood was used as a base for fitting the Spud legs to the pierheads. By D-Day, the Royal Engineers at Marchwood had prepared three miles of floating roadway.

The Solent as a whole built 53 of the Phoenix units, and besides the locations in Southampton, others were made at Stone Point, Stokes Bay, Langstone Harbour, and C Dock and the Floating Dock at Portsmouth. Those built on shore were launched sideways into the water down sloping ramps.

To complete the work, a considerable number of men had to be imported and were thus billeted on local people. By and large, the vast influx of labour into the area was absorbed without problems, although the minutes of the War Emergency Committee in Portsmouth do reveal illwill caused by the 'class of persons' being billeted on the citizens of Southsea. A special camp at Fareham, built to accomodate part of the 'Phoenix' workforce had a hutted canteen to feed 1,000 men – the largest to be erected anywhere in the country by the Ministry of Works.

Mulberry components started their move across the Channel on D-Day itself, and on June 7, the Gooseberries were started by sinking the Corncobs one by one in position. The three breakwaters in the British sector were completed by the 10th, and by the 16th, many of the Phoenix units had been positioned. At Arro-

manches, two floating pierheads were in operation by the 16th, but further tows had been delayed by bad weather. By the 18th, the outlook was more promising and twenty four sections of Whale roadway each 480 feet long set out from the shelter of Spithead. They had not gone far, however, when rising winds forced them to slow down. By the afternoon of the 19th, a full gale was raging, the worst June storm in the Channel for forty years. It lasted for three full days and wreaked havoc on the beaches. Landing craft and Rhino ferries were driven on shore where the wreckage piled up among the stacks of stores. Over 800 smaller vessels were destroyed and the tows of Whales roadway caught in mid-channel were mostly lost at sea.

At Arromanches, most of the outer breakwater held, providing vital shelter to large number of ships and landing craft. At Omaha Beach, however, the incomplete Mulberry was almost totally destroyed and had to be abandoned. Arromanches was soon back in action again, but the storm had gravely threatened the planned build-up of troops and stores in the Normandy beachhead, forcing a temporary lull in the action.

Intelligence gathering

The story began in a hotel swimming pool in Cairo in the early days of 1941. Every morning before the other guests were awake, the lonely figure of Lieutenant-Commander Nigel Clogstoun-Wilmott could be seen swimming length after length of the pool, training himself for long-distance swimming. He was a specialist navigator and a regular naval officer who had already been involved in clandestine operations in Norway.

He was in the Middle East to act as navigating officer to the Commando force which was to occupy the island of Rhodes and had already undertaken a reconnaissance of the proposed landing areas through the periscope of a submarine. This only made him realise, however, that there was to real substitute for an actual examination of a beach and its defences.

It was one thing to have an idea – the problem was, how to carry it out? Clogstoun-Wilmott was introduced to an army lieutenant 'Jumbo' Courtney, who was in Egypt with a small section of Commandos equipped with canoes. The two men trained together for several weeks in the techniques of paddling silently towards a coastline, and then, while one remained in a canoe, the other swam ashore. In those days, the rubber 'wet suit' had not been invented, so to keep out the cold, the swimmers wore pullovers and long underpants liberally coated in periscope grease!

In March 1941, the two men embarked on a submarine and carried out a series of night reconnaissances of the beaches at Rhodes and managed to escape detection. They brought back a lot of useful information about the defences, enemy patrols and the surface of the sand. The actual invasion never took place, owing to the German occupation of Greece, but an idea had been born.

COPP

These initials stood for Combined Operations Assault Pilotage Party, an organisation that was formed under the command of Clogstoun-Wilmott in the late summer of 1942 – to put his beach reconnaissance ideas on a more professional footing. With only eight weeks before the TORCH landings in North Africa, he was ordered to prepare a number of teams to operate with the Allied force and to guide them into the beaches.

A headquarters was set up at the Hayling Island Sailing Club on a lonely beach not far from Portsmouth, and then the real battle started – not with the enemy but with the Royal Navy! There was a desperate need for better canoes and proper swimming suits, but in spite of official orders giving his unit a high degree of priority, Clogstoun-Wilmott was often defeated by naval officers who disliked such 'private armies' in their midst.

Each 'Party' consisted of ten two-man teams who were trained to operate from a canoe – one man was a Royal Navy navigator and the other, a specialist from the Royal Engineers. Training was hard and Clogstoun-Wilmott drove his men to extreme limits of physical exhaustion. Every morning they swam in the sea regardless of the weather and they had to learn to paddle their canoes under storm conditions. By a combination of trickery, bullying and gentle persuasion, better equipment was gradually obtained, and COPP parties were involved with the various Mediterranean landings in 1942 and 1943. They carried out two types of task – firstly, beach reconnaissances as originally envisaged, and secondly, acted as guides to the invasion forces. For the latter case, teams would anchor their canoes just off the beaches to mark the limits of each landing sector and would signal out to sea with shaded lights and infra-red equipment.

The OVERLORD staff had been made aware of the existence of ancient peat workings dating back to Roman times which were located on the beach just to the east of Arromanches – where the British planned to locate their artificial harbour. It was vital to discover the texture of the beach and whether or not it would have to be strengthened before tanks could be driven over it. It was decided that a recce would have to be made and only the most experienced teams would be good enough. Clogstoun-Wilmott decided to lead the operation in person, in spite of his knowledge of the D-Day secret, and after much difficulty was finally given permission to go.

Two specially equipped LCN's (landing craft – navigation) were used, and with COPPs 1 and 2, these were towed to Normandy behind Motor Gun Boats (MGB's). The weather was extremely rough in the Channel in December and the men suffered from sea-sickness while under tow. Outside the range of German radar, the LCN's cast off and moved slowly towards the beach at La Riviere and Ver-sur-Mer – conveniently guided in by the lighthouse which was in operation at the time. Shortly before midnight on 31 December, they were 200 metres off shore and the two swimmers dressed in their bulky suits.

These were made of rubberised fabric and lined with kapok to provide buoyancy. The neck and wrists were sealed by elastic strips and rope-soled 'boots' covered the swimmers' feet. It should be remembered that such suits were designed only for swimming on the surface and were not equipped with underwater breathing apparatus as in the case of 'frogmen'. Each swimmer carried the following items – Waterproof watch and torch, underwater writing tablet and pencils, compass, emergency rations, signal flares and a small flask of Cognac.

The two men who went ashore were Major Scott-Bowden and Sergeant Ogden-Smith, who spent two hours crawling about on the beach in the middle of the various German obstacles. At midnight, the sergeant tapped the major on the shoulder and wished him a Happy New Year! Undiscovered by the enemy, they collected their samples of rock and sand, and made their way safely back to the LCN's. Both of them had felt very exposed on the beach as it was well lit by the revolving beam of the lighthouse.

The information they brought back was most important and proved to the scientists in England that the peat had turned to solid stone. No special precautions had to be taken on that beach. No lives had been lost and the Germans were completely unaware that there had been a landing.

Not long afterwards, however, the services of COPP were to be required once again. Air photographs had shown mysterious coloured stains on the beach that was destined to be Omaha, and there was only one way to find out what they were. For this trip, instead of a LCN, COPP I embarked in an X-class midget submarine as the water off Omaha was deep enough for such a craft to operate safely.

Inside, conditions were most unpleasant. Instead of the normal three-man crew, five men and the swimming equipment had to be packed into a very confined space of less than five metres by three metres – with only one and a half metres headroom! One man could sleep on top of the batteries and another coiled around the engine. They lived mainly on sandwiches, although at night when on the surface, a small stove could provide them with hot soup. During daylight, the submarine had to remain submerged, and then the atmosphere inside soon became unbearable – a mixture of battery acid, diesel fumes, wet clothing and human smells, all combined with a lack of oxygen. The swimmers soon came to the conclusion that they would prefer to face the Germans on the beach than remain inside the submarine!

During the night of 17/18 January 1944, Clogstoun-Wilmott placed the X-craft off Vierville, and the same two swimmers struggled into their suits. In the confined space of the small cabin, this process took two hours and more or less exhausted the men before they even got into the water. Then, they had to climb up onto the narrow deck through a small hatch and squeeze past the captain before lowering themselves into the water.

Once ashore, the two men set out to gather their samples of sand, and to locate on a map where each sample had been taken, they laid out marker lines pegged to the beach.

All was going well, when suddenly footsteps were heard. Scott-Bowden and Ogden-Smith took cover behind the beach obstacles, expecting at any minute to be discovered. A lone German came walking along the beach, stumbled over their marker line and then carried on without noticing that there was anything strange going on.

The recce continued for three more nights along Omaha beach and then the group returned safely to Portsmouth in the submarine, having discovered a lot of useful information – especially the fact that the coloured stains on the sand would not present any problems. At the end of February it was decided to stop the various raids and reconnaissances as the Allies were by then well informed about the beaches and the German defences.

There was, however, one exception to this. Earlier visits as well as air photographs had shown up the existence of a type of defence obstacle known to the Allies as Element-C or Belgian Gate, and it was necessary to examine one of these in detail. In May 1944, a series of small scale raids known under the code-name of 'Tarbrush' were mounted in the Pas de Calais area (Bray Dunes, Onival, Les Hemmes etc) although none of them succeeded in finding any Belgian Gates.

Merchant ships unloading at Southampton.

BUILD-UP

It is difficult to give a precise date when the build-up for Overlord began in the Solent area. As we have already seen, Combined Operations had been in occupation since the Spring of 1942 and their activities were constantly increasing. Parallel to this was the COSSAC planning phase throughout 1943. As early as July 1942, Military Movement Control was established in Southampton with headquarters along side those of the Flag Officer Royal Navy, in the South-Western Hotel. An area extending from Hedge End in the East to Spursholt in the West, running northwards as far as Bushfield Camp at Winchester was designated Area C and placed under the command of a Brigadier.

In the Autumn of that year, an exercise codenamed Cavendish was held to select sites for marshalling camps and to study the road patterns leading to the South. Even before the COSSAC staff was appointed, the build-up of American forces in Britain had begun, under the codename Bolero. Playing a vital role in the operation were the *Queen Mary* and *Queen Elizabeth*. Painted in dull navy grey they shuttled to and fro across the Atlantic unescorted, using their superior speed to evade submarine attack. On each ship it proved possible to accommodate no less than 15,000 troops per journey.

Southampton Docks, already busy with ship repairing, ship building and unloading cargoes from the United States, had to find room for the steadily increasing numbers of landing craft that were being assembled. The Southern Railway Company made every effort to assist the Flag Officer in finding berths, and in addition, lines of piles were driven into the Itchen and mooring buoys were laid wherever there was a spare patch of water.

In the New Docks, berths 105 and 106 became headquarters and stores for the landing craft flotillas. 4th LCT Flotilla was at 49 berth and the 21st LCT Flotilla alongside in the New Docks. Four berths in the Old Docks were occupied by LCI's.

One of the problems posed by landing craft in general, especially those designed to carry vehicles, was loading over the ramps in the bows. This necessitated the use of a slipway or hard, of which there were not enough available. In October 1943, a hard building party was trained at Stokes Bay and put to work in the Portsmouth and Gosport areas.

As far as Southampton was concerned, the following facilities were constructed. Four loading hards built between February 1943 and February 1944 in the docks, plus:

1 slip and 1 grid at Thorneycrofts, Northam. March 1944.
1 slip at Camper and Nicholsons, Northam. September 1943.
2 slips at Crosshouse Wharf, Itchen. August 1943.
2 slips at Cracknore Hard. August 1943.
2 slips at Moody's Yard, Bursledon. April 1944.
2 slips at the ML base, Sarisbury Green. May 1944.
1 slip at HMS *Tormentor*, Warsash. April 1944.

The Docks Manager, Mr H.A. Short, wrote – '. . . the Navy wanted accommodation for craft of all sizes for laying up and repair; the Army had to be satisfied as to berths for their troops to embark, and room for their mechanical transport, equipment and stores; hospital ships, and ships with fresh water for the "operation" had to be accommodated at quays suitable for the purpose. It was also to be borne in mind that eventually the United States Army would want room to ship their troops and

Small US warship alongside a group of LCT's at Berth 101 in the New Docks.

LCT being loaded at S.1 Hard near Berth 101 in the New Docks at Southampton.

Southampton City Museums, Hallett Jerrard Collection

Massed LCT flotillas alongside the New Docks at Southampton.

Southampton City Museums, Hallett Jerrard Collection

LCT's alongside Berth 101 at Southampton, looking across to Marchwood.

Southampton City Museums, Hallett Jerrard Collection

Massed landing craft at Southampton just before D-Day.

Landing Craft Rocket being loaded with projectiles at Southampton.

Southampton City Museums, Hallett Jerrard Collection

D-Day Hard at Crosshouse Wharf on the Itchen River.

Light armour and a self-propelled gun on one of the special hards.

equipment; and with all this the commercial programme had to be maintained . . .'

In April 1943, loading trials with LST's were carried out at S2 and S3 hards in Southampton, and in June, the Woolston end of the floating bridge was requisitioned for the use of Thorneycrofts as a repair base for LCT's and LCI's.

The following month, a major exercise codenamed Harlequin was held using troops, to test the marshalling and embarkation of troops in area C. The results of this secret operation were then to be evaluated by the planners and formed the basis for the camps and the marshalling system that was ultimately evolved for Area C.

Soon, life was to become even more arduous for the local populations of the coastal towns. At noon on 17 August, the whole of the sea front from Southsea through to Eastney was declared a restricted zone and the remaining people living there were cleared out. This was mainly a security measure to shield invasion preparations from prying eyes. The Services' need for accommodation, however, was insatiable. In Portsmouth alone, billeting had to be found for 29,000 extra personnel – not including troops to be embarked for Overlord. Hotels and boarding houses were requisitioned en masse and local schools were occupied in the absence of their evacuated pupils and staff. Eight tented camps for 500 men each were set up at different places on Portsea Island, and the various naval shore bases were crammed to bursting point. It was the same story in Southampton, where ever warehouses in the docks were converted into sleeping quarters. The National Provincial Bank in Canute Road was converted into barracks as well as most of the schools, including the Girls Grammar School and the King Edward VI School. Tauntons School served for most of the war as a camp for German prisoners, before being handed over to the Americans after D-Day. Other units had to be housed as far afield as the Grand Hotel at Lyndhurst.

During the Autumn of 1943, work was started in earnest to create the necessary infrastructure to receive, house and embark the troops destined for the initial landing as well as the follow-up divisions. The sailing capacity of Southampton was fixed at 11,000 troops on each of the four daily tides, and the capacity of Area C was laid down as 44,000 troops (four times the port capacity) and 6,270 vehicles. Ultimately twenty five special camps were built with tented accommodation divided into blocks of 500 men. In addition, wooden huts were provided to serve as cook-houses, dining halls, ablutions blocks, chapels, NAAFI facilities etc.

These camps were constructed by the military authorities who were also responsible for the provision of the necessary roadways, water connections and hard standing for vehicles. The main camp in Area C occupied the whole of Southampton Common, which had been similarly used during the First World War. Another was just outside Romsey, in the woods to the north of Winchester Road. For troops embarking from Portsmouth, the main concentration area was tucked away in the woods on Butser Hill, while another large camp was situated at Titchfield. Besides their responsibility for Southampton Docks, the Southern Railway Company became involved in a programme of special works directly connected with Overlord which cost almost one million pounds. Vast new sidings had to be constructed to accommodate trains carrying both troops and stores of all kinds. The marshalling yard at Eastleigh, for example, was mainly built to cope with pre-D-Day military traffic, and the rail network inside the docks was similarly extended.

In March Vera Brittain visited her holiday cottage in the New Forest and noted in her diary – 'At every turn of every glade we found waggons and ammunition dumps, vainly sought by Nazi observers, which the late-budding trees concealed. Our nights echoed to the ceaseless clatter of heavy tanks lumbering down the Bournemouth-Southampton road'.

American vehicle column parked in Southampton Docks waiting for shipment.

Southampton City Museums, Hallett Jerrard Collection

THE NEPTUNE PLAN AS IT APPLIED TO THE REGION

The final version of Neptune, the assault phase of Overlord, was approved on 1 February 1944 and the postponement to early June was agreed. As far as the Solent area was concerned, the bulk of the three British assault forces were to be assembled and to sail from there. On 17 May, General Eisenhower selected 5 June as D-Day, and the ideal was to land the troops as soon as possible after dawn on a three-quarters tide. Each assault force was destined for one of the British beaches –

Force S – Sword Beach – 3rd Infantry Division
Force J – Juno Beach – 3rd Canadian Infantry Division
Force G – Gold Beach – 50th Infantry Division.

The Headquarters for Force S was at Commercial Buildings in Portsmouth, for Force J at Cowes Castle, the home of the Royal Yacht Squadron, and for Force G in the South-Western Hotel.

Each Force was to be accompanied by a Bombarding Force –
Force K to support Assault Force G. HQ ship HMS *Argonaut*
Force E to support Assault Force J. HQ ship HMS *Belfast*
Force D to support Assault Force S. HQ ship HMS *Mauritius*.

All the above units were combined as the Eastern Naval Task Force commanded by Rear Admiral Sir Phillip Vian in HMS *Scylla*.

The heavy guns were provided by the battleships *Warspite* and *Ramilles*, the monitor HMS *Roberts*, with *Rodney* in reserve.

The aim was for the convoys to sail from their various embarkation ports at staggered intervals and move along the coast in lanes regularly kept clear of mines, where it was hoped that they would not excite too much interest. The rendezvous point was Area Z, popularly known as Piccadilly Circus, a few miles south of the Isle of Wight. From there the task forces would form up and move south behind a screen of minesweepers and then turn in towards the Normandy Coast. Six or seven miles offshore, the bombarding forces would take up position and the landing craft mother ships would unload the smaller craft for the journey ashore. Behind the assault formations was Force L, the follow up group which was already loaded and could be disembarked as soon as a foothold on the beaches had been gained.

Because of the shortage of landing craft and the confined area on the actual landing beaches, each assault division would take only about forty per cent of its vehicles and a bare minimum of equipment. Once on shore, units would then be gradually completed as ships brought in further men, stores and ammunition according to a planned sequence. Thus every ship and boat load had to be tailored with regard to its destination and proposed use. Inevitably there were mistakes and the odd unit desperately needing mortar bombs received 500 cases of marmalade instead. By and large, however, one of the miracles of the whole operation was the way in which the logistic back-up functioned so perfectly – a credit to the army of anonymous planners and load masters who made it all possible.

Another aspect of the support plan was the use of landing craft to provide additional fire-power on the run-in to the beaches. Some were fitted with field guns, forming amphibious batteries, while the tanks loaded in other vessels were programmed to fire inshore as soon as they came within range of the German defences. The Landing Craft Flak (LCF) were fitted with anti-aircraft guns and the Landing Craft Rocket (LCR) with multi-barrel rocket launchers. The latter were christened the 'Flying Mattress' and were used to drench shore positions with salvoes of high explosive projectiles.

American locomotive en route for Normandy being prepared for loading on to one of the Southern Railway train ferries at Southampton Docks.

COUNT-DOWN

We have seen that at the beginning of 1944, the Supreme Commander had been appointed and General Montgomery was on his way back to England to take command of 21st Army Group. Along the South Coast, thousands of men were engaged in construction of Mulberry Harbour units, Pluto pipes and other hardware. Portsmouth, Southampton and lesser inlets were already crowded with landing craft, which were being added to by the week. So crowded was Britain becoming that Eisenhower was to quip that the only thing stopping the island from sinking under the weight was the mass of barrage balloons holding it up.

The arrival of the Americans
During the assault phase, only British and Commonwealth troops were to be processed through Southampton and Portsmouth, but afterwards, both harbours were to handle the bulk of the American follow-up forces and their stores. As early as July 1943, a small advanced party of 14th Major Port, United States Army Transportation Corps, arrived in Southampton, initially responsible for cargo handling. Ultimately they were to be in charge of American port operations all along the coast between Weymouth and Newhaven. The enlisted men of this advance party were quartered in the Ascupart Road School and the officers at the Polygon Hotel. By February, the number of US personnel had grown to such an extent that the enlisted men had been moved out to Blighmont Barracks, now the T.A. Centre at Totton. Their main headquarters was established on 1 February at Maritime Chambers in the Old Docks. In May it was transferred to one wing of the Civic Centre.

It was also planned that the marshalling camps in Area C would be jointly administered and guarded by British and American troops on a fifty-fifty basis. The American contingent was provided by the 29th Infantry Regiment which arrived in the area in March 1944. Its headquarters had to be set up as far away as Ampfield House near Romsey.

Attached to 14th Major Port were a number of units known as Harbor Craft Companies, whose job was to operate the myriad fleet of tugs, lighters, floating cranes and other small craft attached to the local ports. They were quartered at Swaythling Infants School through most of 1944. At Richard Taunton's School, the prisoner of war camp was moved out and a number of subsidiary American units took over. Among these were the Ambulance Companies whose job was to ferry the wounded from the incoming hospital ships to trains and to local casualty stations. In this respect, the vast military hospital complex at Netley, the Royal Victoria Hospital, was almost entirely taken over by the American forces. So generous were the dimensions of the now sadly demolished hospital, that it was said that the Americans drove jeeps along the ground floor corridors.

A further major United States organisation was the Naval Advanced Amphibious Base which arrived in May and was given the Star Hotel as headquarters. Additional living space was created in a hutted camp at the bottom of the High Street. With a complement of 65 officers and 800 enlisted men, this unit was responsible for providing logistic support for US Naval forces in the Portsmouth–Southampton area, for repairing American vessels operating an engineering and signal office at Calshot and a VHF radio station on the Isle of Wight.

For recreation, various facilities had to be provided for the

RAMC personnel on parade on 15 January 1944 when Netley hospital was handed over to the Americans.

Travellers' identity cards being checked at Fratton station after the ban on entry to the coastal area.

US column at Berth 107 in Southampton Docks.

Southampton City Museums, Hallett Jerrard Collection

influx of American personnel. In Portsmouth, the American Red Cross were able to open a recreation centre at the Hilsea Lido cafe – in spite of some local opposition, and in Southampton, the Bargate Club was a popular facility. Catching the spirit of this friendly invasion, scores of ordinary citizens in the area made the newcomers welcome, taking them into their homes, making cups of tea for the men on the columns of vehicles parked along the verges and providing hot water for shaving. There was friction from time to time, but by and large the two communities decided to simply like each other. After the war, General Eisenhower wrote – '. . . people cheerfully accepted of using their own streets and roads at the risk of being run down, of seeing their fields and gardens trampled, of waiting in long queues for trains that never arrived, and of suffering a further cut in an already meagre ration so that nothing should interfere with the movement of soldiers and the mountains of supplies we so lavishly consumed'.

Further restrictions

On 31 March 1944, the Secretary of State for War issued Regulated Area (No. 2) Order, to come into force at noon the following day. This established a ten mile deep strip of land inwards from the coast, stretching from the Wash to Lands End, which was closed to all visitors. In addition, foreign diplomatic missions in England were prohibited from making radio transmissions. Within the restricted area itself, local residents also found their movements curtailed and subjected to snap controls at all times. Permanent guards were established at railway stations, bus depots and roads leading into the zone from outside. At the Isle of Wight ferry terminals, notices were posted, signed by Lieutenant-General William Morgan, C.O.C. Southern Command, stating that nobody who was not a resident on the Island could take passage on the steamers. The month before, 141 Infantry Brigade under the command of Brigadier Hanney was moved down from Scotland to take over as garrison for Area C.

One of their tasks, together with their American counterparts, was to surround the marshalling camps with barbed-wire fences. Once the troops had moved in and been briefed, there was to be only one way out of the area – onto a ship and down the Solent towards France.

By April, 'Southampton had become one vast camp, dump and airfield. Every bit of woodland, every copse accessible from the road was packed with lorries and jeeps. The woods on the Downs at Beauworth were a vast ammunition dump . . .'.

Headquarters established.

The final phase of preparation can really be said to have started on 26 April. On that date, Admiral Ramsey's ANCXF head-

The planning map in the war room at Southwick House (now HMS Dryad*) which has been preserved as a relic of the operation that was launched from there.*

Canadians on board a Landing Craft Assault during Exercise Fabius.

Public archives of Canada

quarters moved into Southwick House, just to the north of Portsmouth. At the same time, an advanced party from St. Pauls School, set up Montgomery's Tactical HQ in the grounds. This consisted of a number of caravans which were parked under a clump of trees to provide camouflage. Major Paul Odgers was responsible for this small well organised unit which Monty had perfected in North Africa and Italy, enabling him to command near the front line and away from the routine staff work in 21st Army Group Main HQ. Odgers wrote – 'The whole outfit was in tents, . . . with a marquee for Monty's dining room. He himself was living in Broomfield House, and didn't come to the head-quarters except to meet the officers . . .' For the next few weeks the staff practiced the complicated procedure of packing up and moving the whole headquarters, driving 30 miles out into the Sussex countryside and then returning to Southwick. By D-Day, they were a well rehearsed team ready to go to war in France. Monty himself spent most of April visiting the various units which he would command in battle. On 9 April he witnessed an exercise carried out by the 3rd Canadian Division at Studland Bay for example, mounted from their HQ at Brockenhurst.

He used these visits to deliver roistering pep talks to the men. His jeep would drive up, and standing on the bonnet, the general would ask the troops to gather round and 'stand easy'. He was easily the best known figure after the Prime Minister in England at the time, and with his natural gifts as a showman, he spoke to his soldiers in a language that they could both appreciate and understand.

Concentration

Generally speaking, the various movement orders for the assault units to move into their concentration areas went out at the end of April, although due to the sheer numbers involved, this was staggered over a period of several weeks and was combined with a number of dress rehearsals for the landings. Not all formations who took part in the dress rehearsals stayed in the area after-wards – some were sent back to their intermediate staging areas. By April, however, most troops involved in the initial phases of the landings had been brought south of a line from the Wash to Milford Haven.

For example, 3rd Canadian Division with headquarters in Brockenhurst, was spread between Boscombe and Milford on Sea, and 1st Special Services Brigade made up of various Com-mando units was based around Midhurst with its headquarters at Cowdrey Park.

The rehearsals were given the code-name Fabius and each assault force was marshalled, embarked and practiced a landing on a section of the coast –

Force G on Hayling Island
Force J at Bracklesham Bay
Force S at Littlehampton.

No 48 Commando Royal Marines was a comparatively new unit, having been specially formed to take part in Overlord as part of No 4 Special Services Brigade. Their mission was to land at St. Aubin on Juno Beach and move along the coast to take the strongpoint at Langrune-sur-Mer. On 29 April they moved from their billets at Gravesend in Kent, to C3 Marshalling Camp at Botley. Few of the men were aware that this was to be an exercise, and the three days at Botley were spent in waterproof-ing vehicles. All the men were briefed that the area of Brack-lesham Bay represented an enemy coastline and they were to land behind a Canadian Regiment (The North Shore Regiment), wheel to the left and 'attack' West Wittering.

Early on the morning of 3 May, the commando was driven in lorries to Warsash where they embarked in the Landing Craft Infantry (Small) (LCI(S)) of 202 Flotilla. The rest of the day was spent practising disembarking in Stanswood Bay, a man-

Exercise Fabius. Assault units landing in Bracklesham Bay.

Public archives of Canada

44

Canadian RAM tanks coming ashore during Exercise Fabius.

Vehicles being unloaded from an LCT in Bracklesham Bay during Exercise Fabius. In the foreground are Universal Carriers adapted to transport water.

Public archives of Canada

LCT flotilla in the Old Docks at Southampton.

Southampton City Museums, Hallett Jerrard Collection

The New Docks entirely filled with LCT's. In the background are the Solent Flour Mills.

Dry Dock used as a parking bay for landing craft at Southampton. There was even time to hang out the washing.

Southampton City Museums, Hallett Jerrard Collection

Tea parade in the woods 'somewhere in area C'.

oeuvre that the men found difficult as the LCI(S) did not have a ramp at the front. The only way to get off was to clamber down narrow gangways.

The night was spent at sea in the Channel, minus the LCT which was to have carried the unit transport. It had run aground and could not be refloated, so the vehicles had to proceed by road. The landing the following morning in Bracklesham Bay was a success, however, and by 1120 hours, the defences of Wittering had been mopped up.

Also involved in the Fabius series was the 10th Canadian Armoured Regiment (The Fort Garry Horse), equipped with Sherman DD tanks. They had spent the winter at Milford on Sea, and in March they were split up. Two squadrons moved to a hideout at Fawley while the rest of the regiment was quartered at Fort Gomer near Gosport. The vehicles were parked at Lee on Solent. In April, the whole unit was reunited when the two squadrons from Fawley moved to Fort Monkton and Bay House, where they were inspected by the King on 25 April. At this stage, all the troops had a pretty good idea that they would be going to invade the Continent, but generally speaking, only their senior commanders had been given some indication of the plans they would have to carry out.

Also hidden away in the woods behind Fawley and Hythe (the Shangri-La camp) was the 231 Brigade of 50th Northumbrian Division, destined to land on Gold Beach as the spearhead of Force G. When they marched to Southampton to embark for the Fabius rehearsal, the local people, believing they were off to war, handed out precious sweets and cigarettes. So well was the secret kept apparently, that when they returned to the city for the real embarkation, they were given nothing – the locals regarding it as just another practice. Thus by early May, the assault units of Force G were concentrated to the west of Southampton Water and back into the New Forest. 3rd Canadian Division, or Force J was in a string of camps between Chilworth to the north of Southampton and the shore of Stokes Bay. Force S was spread in an arc to the north and east of Portsmouth – between Waterlooville and Emsworth.

The necessary shipping had also been concentrated by the end of April, when Force G arrived in the Southampton area from Portland on the 28th. The Flag Officer's records show the following assembly areas –

Force G

1	LSH at 41 berth	
135	LCT, LCM and LCA in New Docks	
25	LCM and Nos. 2 and 3 trots.	
14	ML's in Inner Docks	
7	LCF	At buoys in the Beaulieu River
6	LCG (L)	,, ,,
16	LCT (A)	,, ,,
8	LCT (R)	,, ,,

Force J

24	LCT at buoys at Calshot
30	LCT in Ocean Dock
25	LCT in Empress Dock
10	LCT in Outer Dock
35	LCT at Berths 34, 35 and 36
60	LCT and A, B, C, D, and E trots.
10	LCS (L) at Redbridge and No. 1 trot
8	LCH at Town Quay
22	ML's at Berths 43
4	LSI at Berths 37, 38, 39 and 40.
	LCF at Berths 49 and 50

The Fabius exercises were designed to be as realistic as possible, and during and after the briefings, the troops were sealed in. Each camp was entirely surrounded by wire which was guarded by patrolling sentries both inside and outside. Movements between camps were carried out under guard and the only people allowed in and out were subject to close scrutiny.

King George VI inspecting a naval guard. Copyright 'The News', Portsmouth

Armoured column parked in Horndean. Copyright 'The News', Portsmouth

Column of Sherman tanks in Portchester Road, en route to the harbour. Copyright 'The News', Portsmouth

REME personnel playing cards in one of the marshalling camps prior to D-Day. Copyright 'The News', Portsmouth

FINALE

On 5 May, Admiral Ramsay issued orders that no further alterations in the Neptune plan would be permitted. The various shortcomings that had been thrown up during Fabius had been eliminated as far as possible, and all concerned were satisfied with the plans. On 15 May, a final presentation was held at St. Pauls School in the presence of the King, the Prime Minister, General Smuts and the British Chiefs of Staff. Two days later, Eisenhower finally confirmed 5 June as the date of D-Day. From then on, the whole operation took on a momentum of its own as the well rehearsed plans were implemented. Ships, men, vehicles and stores moved to an exact timetable, until on 26 May, the camps were sealed off from the outside world for the last time. Eisenhower moved down to his advanced HQ in the woods near Southwick House to be close to Montgomery and Ramsey.

One of the signs according to the old soldiers, of impending action was a visit from 'the big shots'. The Chaplain of the North Shore Regiment in the marshalling camp at Chilworth, wrote – '. . . we marched out to the field one hot day and stood for nearly two hours; then a whisper ran along the line: "It's the King," and quietly, King George the Sixth walked through the lines as the band played on. A few days later, in the same field, General Montgomery, with all the showmanship that helps to make him the great leader of men he is, stood up on a jeep, called the men around him and, like an old-fashioned auctioneer, spoke of the task ahead. A few days later, Eisenhower, on his off-hand American manner, which we all liked, strolled through the lines, smiled, and spoke to a man here and there and wished us the best'.

During this final waiting period, the assault units occupied themselves with shedding personnel and equipment they would not be taking to France with them. Kit was packed up and sent back to depots for safe-keeping. First line reinforcements (seven percent of war establishment) were sent to holding camps, one of which was at Popham, just to the north of Winchester. From there they could be sent over to France to replace casualties incurred during the actual landings. Unit vehicles were pre-loaded with stores, ammunition and petrol, and were sent to hard standings near the various embarkation points. One carriageway of the Winchester by-pass was closed to traffic and became a vast tank park, with vehicles stretched nose to tail for miles.

One major problem was concealment. With so much packed into such a relatively small area of the country, German aircraft would have had a field day. Admittedly the Allies had achieved total air superiority by that stage of the war but there was always the danger of the odd raider sneaking through. The various marshalling camps were tucked away in woods as far as possible and great use of camouflage netting was made – the Avenue leading into Southampton became one long leafy tunnel as the spaces between the existing trees were covered with netting. Barrage balloons were hoisted above the flotillas of landing craft to hinder low-flying aircraft, and both Portsmouth and Southampton became blanketed by smoke screens. The often acrid-smelling smoke was not appreciated by the local inhabitants.

25 May was the last night of liberty for the troops. No 48 Commando travelled down by rail from Gravesend that day, to arrive at Swaythling Station. From there they went to C19 Marshalling Camp which was situated on the Common. 'That night

Canadian troops on landing craft in the Old Docks at Southampton just before leaving for France. *Public archives of Canada*

American LCT and a DUKW amphibian off the entrance to Portsmouth harbour. *Copyright 'The News', Portsmouth*

the camp was left open and the fortunate ones found their last glass of beer for several months'.

Lord Lovat, in command of 1st Special Service Brigade, described the scene – 'Whistling "Lilli Burlero", formations . . . debussed in the suburbs of Southampton. They did not arrive together, but a distinctive appearance was common to them all. There was, perhaps, a hint of arrogance in that first impression . . . They looked good and they damn well knew it. The assembly area, scene of some confusion, already swarmed with bewildered infantry, sitting round piled arms with that far-from-home and nowhere-to-go cast of countenance that characterises troops in transit!' Once the camps had been sealed, briefing began in detail for the first time with the aid of maps and remarkably detailed models of the assault areas. At this stage, however, no names were mentioned 'in clear' and every place was known only by a code-word (St. Aubin-sur-Mer became Cairo). All correspondence and phone-calls were stopped, and telegrams could only be sent for urgent compassionate reasons. Any bodies of troops who had to leave camp were escorted by armed guards.

Inside the barbed wire, there was plenty to do. A NAAFI tent dispensed sweets and soft drinks, there was a cinema tent and some units organised sports events. Lord Lovat's commandos did not suffer from boredom – 'Officers busied themselves with final arrangements and the check-ups that save lives- dinghies were inflated, bayonets sharpened, automatic springs tested, magazines oiled, waterproof wrapping wound round all weapons, escape maps were issued together with ammunition, rations and first aid kits. Hand grenades were not primed until the day of departure'. One military formality was the handing out of will forms, to be filled in and deposited with the camp

South Wales Borderers ready to embark at Southsea.

administration officers. The chaplains of all denominations were also busy.

The Reverend Hickey, Roman Catholic padré to the North Shore Regiment, referred to his job as providing 'spiritual water-proofing'. 'I've never felt more satisfied in my life than the night before the Invasion; for, like all the other chaplains, I had the consolation to know that every one of my men had been perso-nally contacted and given an opportunity to receive the sacra-ments'.

The X-craft depart.
Initially all looked set for D-Day as planned on 5 June, and some units were already embarking vehicles and stores as early as 28 May. On the afternoon of 2 June, two X class midget submarines left their base at HMS Dolphin at Gosport, under tow for the Normandy coast. X-20 and X-23 were to be the first Allied vessels to take up position off France and their task was to mark the way for the main invasion fleet. Once on station they were to remain submerged during daylight and finally surface shortly before H-hour. X-23 was to mark the eastern extremity of Sword Beach off Ouistreham, and X-20 the western limit of Gold Beach off Le Hamel near Arromanches.

Each vessel carried its normal navy crew of three, plus two specialists from the COPP team to act as navigators. The sub-marines were equipped with collapsible 18 feet high masts which could show a shaded light only visible from the sea as well as an automatic radio signal. In addition to such technical aids, they used a somewhat more primitive device known as the 'bong stick'. This was a form of mechanical hammer acting on the bottom of the sea which sent out a rhythmic sound capable of being picked up on the fleet's Asdic equipment. It was operated by one of the COPP men sitting on the forward casing with his legs dangling in the water. By the morning of Sunday, 4 June, they were on station and unaware that D-Day had been post-poned. Cautiously, Lieutenant George Honour raised the peri-scope of X-23 and checked his position by the prominent church spires along the shore. He observed French people walking to church and German soldiers on the beach. All was quiet.

The weather crisis
On 1 June, Admiral Ramsey assumed command of the forces engaged in Operation Neptune and general operational control in the Channel. Everything then hinged on the weather, and it was agreed that Eisenhower and the other commanders would meet regularly to consider the forecasts. These meetings took place in the library at Southwick House, described by Cornelius Ryan as 'a large comfortable room with a table covered by a green baize cloth, several easy chairs and two sofas. Dark oak

bookcases lined three of the walls, but there were few books on the shelves and the room had a bare look. Heavy double black-out curtains hung at the windows and . . . muffled the drumming of the rain and the flat buckling sound of the wind.'

Throughout May the weather had been excellent, but by 2 June when the commanders met, there were strong indications that the fine spell was going to end. However, it was decided to proceed. Bombarding Force D sailed from the Clyde and HMS *Nelson* left Scapa Flow.

The following morning brought low cloud, strong winds and steadily increasing waves. Bombarding Forces E and K also left the Clyde, and late in the afternoon, the spearhead of the American assault forces left several Devon ports – part of Force U which had the furthese distance to travel to the assembly point south of the Isle of Wight. That evening, the weather meeting was confronted by an extremely pessimistic forecast and a post-ponement was definitely on the cards. Eisenhower, however, upon whose shoulders lay the burden of making the final deci-sion, decided to wait for one more forecast.

At 4 am on the morning of 4 June, it was obvious that a storm would be raging on the following day and the Supreme Comman-der, with deep regret, ordered a 24 hour postponement. Im-mediately signals were sent to stop the forces which had already sailed. A flotilla of 'Corncobs' had to seek shelter off Poole and Force U anchored in Weymouth Bay. Those troops who had already embarked in Portsmouth and Southampton were brought back ashore if their ships were still tied up to the quays, but the unlucky ones who were already at anchor in Spithead, passed an extremely uncomfortable day and night.

At 9.30 in the evening, the weather meeting reconvened. Present were Eisenhower, Montgomery, Air Chief Marshal Ted-der, Admiral Ramsey, Air Chief Marshal Leigh-Mallory and General Bedell Smith, Ike's chief-of-staff. The atmosphere was

The embarkation staff at Southsea, apparently under the command of a wing commander in the RAF. Copyright 'The News', Portsmouth

by all accounts, grim, when the meteorologists entered, led by Group Captain Stagg of the RAF. It fell to the latter to offer a ray of hope to the assembled officers as he indicated an unex-pected change in the prevailing weather pattern. A new front had been observed which would move up Channel and cause the weather over the beaches to clear on the 5th, continuing through to the 6th. At the same time the wind would drop appreciably. Thus the conditions expected were still hardly ideal but did offer a prospect of success.

Stagg and his colleagues were eagerly cross-questioned and then asked to leave the room. Alone with his commanders, Eisenhower solicited their opinions. The person with the greatest problems of a practical nature was Ramsay. If his forces sailed and were again recalled, many ships would have to refuel – for which no provision had been made. One by one the various

Winston Churchill visits Southampton just before D-Day.

Southampton City Museums, Hallett Jerrard Collection

Herbert Morrison inspecting fire brigade vehicles in Southampton on 24 May 1944.

Copyright 'The News', Portsmouth

commanders gave their opinions, the majority being in favour of going ahead on the sixth. Cornelius Ryan described the scene thus – 'It was now up to Ike. The moment had come when only he could make the decision. There was a long silence as Eisenhower weighed all the possibilities. General Smith, watching, was struck by the "isolation and loneliness" of the Supreme Commander as he sat, hands clasped before him, looking down at the table. The minutes ticked by; some say two minutes passed, others as many as five. Then Eisenhower, his face strained, looked up and announced his decision. Slowly he said, "I am quite positive we must give the order . . . I don't like it, but there it is . . . I don't see how we can do anything else" '.

The arrival of the Prime Minister
While this drama was being played out in the library of South-

wick House, another actor had entered the stage. On 3 June, Winston Churchill's special train parked in the cutting at Droxford Station. The old warrior wanted to be in on the final scene and had fully intended to take part in the invasion itself. That notion had been firmly squashed by the combined pressure of Eisenhower, Montgomery and even the King. Therefore he had to be content with the role of spectator and spent the afternoon of the 3rd with General Smuts and Ernest Bevin, at Southampton docks, viewing the embarkation, after which, he cruised down the Solent in a launch. This excursion was followed by a visit to Eisenhower.

Commander Harry Butcher, Eisenhower's aide noted in his diary – 'Returning to camp last night, the PM's caravan of cars and dashing cyclists swirled in behind, unexpectedly. Filled their petrol tanks and diminished our supply of Scotch, there being

British troops embarking at South Parade Pier, Southsea. They are led by a private in the Royal Engineers, one of the embarkation staff.

Royal Engineers embarking from South Parade Pier along a special causeway made up from scaffolding poles.

Embarkation pier on Southsea beach. In the background is the line of obstacles reaching out to Spitbank Fort.

Churchill tanks being loaded on to a LST down a concrete hard.

some ten or more parched mouths to moisten . . .'

On the morning of the 4th, the Prime Minister received a visitor at Droxford. General de Gaulle had been flown in from Algeria, to be told that the Allies proposed to invade his country two days later. Although the meeting started cordially enough, over lunch it degenerated into a slanging match. The main point of disagreement was that the Allies proposed to circulate military currency in France, which de Gaulle refused to accept. Later, he was taken to see Eisenhower at his caravan in the woods, where there was a further disagreement. The prickly leader of the Free French was shown the draft of a speech that Ike proposed to broadcast to France on D-Day, which made no mention of himself or his movement. Somewhat surprised by the vehemence of de Gaulle's objections, the Supreme Commander agreed to consider revision of the speech.

Embarkation

The soldiers, sailors and airmen involved had no inkling of the problems of their superiors. Their destiny was simply in the hands of Military Movement Control, which processed them like some giant factory.

On the morning of 5 June, Eisenhower drove down to South Parade Pier at Southsea to visit British troops embarking on LCI's 600, 601 and 602. All along the Southsea beach, lines of men laden with equipment shuffled down to the waiting craft. To get them on board, piers made from scaffolding poles had been constructed, leading down to the edge of the water from the sea wall. By this time, Portsmouth Harbour was almost empty. The flotillas of minesweepers were already at sea making for the lanes which they would have to clear, and HMS *Hornet* at Gosport, the Coastal Forces base had despatched its MTB's to cover the flanks of the assault force from surprise attacks by German E Boats and destroyers.

During the night of 3 June, the Canadian 10th Armoured Regiment received their orders to embark –

'We left the Fort Gomer area, mounted our tanks, and were soon moving off towards the Hards. Craft were packed with an odd assortment of tanks, infantry carriers, anti-tank guns, trucks and jeeps. Our column crawled through the sleeping town of Alverstoke during the night and embarked at about 0800 hours on the Hards near Bay House on 4th June or, as it later transpired to be, D minus 2 Day. We moved up the Solent and tied up to buoys in Southampton Water. We were not allowed off the craft but the sights about us were engrossing and stimulating; landing craft of all sorts were heavily laden with troops and equipment; ex-Cross Channel steamers filled with infantry moved down stream and fast Royal Navy motor launches sped about.'

Most of the two brigades of Commandos embarked at Warsash, and were taken there in trucks on 5 June from the marshalling camp on Southampton Common. The convoys drove out through Bitterne, along the Bursledon Road and turned off at Sarisbury Green. Local people had become inured to the sight of processions of trucks along their suburban roads, but almost everyone seemed to sense that this was not just another exercise.

Through the afternoon of the 5th, the flotillas of landing craft left their harbours and headed out into the Solent. The men on board faced an unpleasant night at sea and the prospect of battle at dawn – for many of them their first taste of combat. Lieutenant-Colonel Moulton, commanding 48 Commando Royal Marines wrote – 'Then down the Hamble and into the Solent. It was crowded with ships and craft of all the various types for the invasion. Every craft and ship seemed to be full of men in khaki, in great spirits, exchanging cheers and jeers, as we and others passed. In the fickle sunshine, in our smart fast craft, wearing our green berets, we and the other commandos were on

Canadians being briefed by an officer on board ship with a map of the assault area.
Public archives of Canada

Religious service on the deck of a ship in the Solent, prior to leaving for Normandy.
Public archives of Canada

A young warrant officer writing home, perched on a loaded jeep.
Public archives of Canada

top of the world. The sun set and we headed for the Nab Tower. It grew colder and the waves grew bigger. We went below out of the cold and the sailors brought supper'.

The North Shore Regiment was one of the units which embarked in Southampton Docks on the 3rd June on the *Brigadier*, converted into an LSI, which then proceeded to anchor off Cowes. There they were caught by the postponement. Their chaplain wrote – 'Sunday morning I said Mass in the mens' quarters. I never expect to have a more attentive congregation than I had that morning; neither do I ever hope to preach with more conviction'.

Another Canadian witness wrote of the 5th June – 'That afternoon, the mighty Armada began to move out; all the way down to the boom opposite Portsmouth, the water was thick with warships, transports and landing craft. Some carried the scarlet band denoting our 3rd Canadian Division Naval Force 'J',

others belonged to Force 'S' with the 3rd British Division who were to land on our left. After we passed through the boom, the real maps were issued and studied and a special message from General Montgomery was issued and read. A short 'O' group was held by the commanding officer on the quarter deck of his craft, interrupted by some unfortunates already having to rush to the side'.

Forces J and S left the sheltering lee of the Isle of Wight via the Nab Tower, while Force G used the Needles Channel. Once outside the various craft encountered a force 5 wind and choppy seas. From there all the craft proceeded to Area Z or Piccadilly Circus where they were marshalled into groups for the passage down the swept channels towards the French coast. There, they were joined by the bombarding forces which had left the Clyde two days before.

LCT's waiting to move off for Normandy in a choppy sea. Note the barrage balloons flying above.

Copyright 'The News', Portsmouth

Railway trucks being loaded into a LST at Southampton.
Southampton City Museums, Hallett Jerrard Collection

German prisoners from Normandy being marched past Dock Gate No. 8.
Southampton City Museums, Hallett Jerrard Collection

The western end of the docks at Southampton viewed from the deck of the Twickenham Ferry. *Southampton City Museums, Hallett Jerrard Collection*

US forces loading vehicles on to a transporter alongside the New Docks, Southampton.
Southampton City Museums, Hallett Jerrard Collection

AFTERMATH

The sailing of the assault convoys did not by any means signify the end of the operation for the Solent area. Just behind, the lumbering groups of tugs towing the Mulberry Harbour units cleared Stokes Bay and Southampton Water according to a precise schedule that was to continue for several days. Until Pluto could be brought into operation, all fuel would have to be delivered by tanker to the beaches. Most of our oil products arrived in this country on the West Coast and were fed by pipelines to the main distribution and refining centres. The major junction on this system was at Aldermaston, and from there a pipeline ran to the Solent area which was ultimately extended as far as the Isle of Wight Pluto pumping stations. A branch led to the Shell-Mex and BP oil terminal at Hamble, the main pier of which had been extended before D-Day. This was used both for refuelling ships on the spot and loading the small tankers that plied between the Solent and the actual invasion beaches. On 5 June, for example, 212 vessels were bunkered at the Hamble jetty.

As far as Portsmouth was concerned, once the assault phase was over, its naval base returned to its traditional role. Southampton, however, awoke to a new life. As the British troops vacated the marshalling camps, the Americans moved in and took over. From then until the end of the war, the city and its docks were to be the main US shipment port for the whole of the United Kingdom.

The initial task was to feed the follow-up divisions into Normandy and to cope with the immense build-up of vehicles and stores required for the break-out towards the Seine. As an example, between D-Day and 23 September, the port of Southampton handled 1,002,955 tons of cargo – roughly the same amount as the entire import and export tonnage in 1939.

Under Operation Bolero which got underway as early as 1942, the Americans had been building up their own system of holding camps and storage depots. One of the latter was at Lockerley near Romsey with a total area of 450,240 square feet of covered storage space. Rail sidings connected directly to the Southampton-Salisbury line and thus to the docks.

Main element in the US forces build-up was the Third Army under the command of General George Patton which was due to join First Army in France in July. Patton's presence was a closely guarded secret and part of the massive deception plan to persuade the enemy that the invasion would come in the Pas de Calais. In Kent, simulated radio traffic, fake airfields, inflatable tanks and a horde of other deceptive measures were to trick the German intelligence authorities into believing that Patton was commanding an army group there. In fact, Patton's advance headquarters was established shortly before D-Day at Braemore House near Fordingbridge in the New Forest. On 4 July, Patton and his staff arrived in Southampton to embark for France – worried that the war would be over before they could get into action.

Handling all this traffic was the 14th Major Port and its host of associated units, labour companies, truck companies, ambulance columns and railway specialists – all working closely with the Southern Railway and the Docks administration. On 21 July, they had their busiest day – 75 ships were loaded for France with 10,603 tons of cargo and nearly 20,000 troops. Many youngsters from Southampton remember profiting from the departing Americans who would often hand out their remaining English money – as well as the inevitable chewing gum.

German general being escorted ashore at Southampton by American MP's.

Southampton City Museums, Hallett Jerrard Collection

Also in July, Colonel Sherman L Kiser took over as Port Commandant, remaining in that position until the US base was deactivated a year later. In a closing down message to his staff, he listed a number of important milestones –

25 October 44	the millionth US serviceman left Southampton for France.
27 October 44	22,465 troops shipped during a single 24 hour period.
12 November 44	Weymouth-Poole activated as sub-port 'C'.
2 February 45	US troops granted leave started to return from the Continent via Southampton.
24 March 45	Hamble sub-port shipped its half-millionth ton of petroleum products.
8 May 45	Victory in Europe Day
23 June 45	Staging areas opened at Tidworth and Barton Stacey to receive troops returning to the United States
25 August 45	*Queen Elizabeth* sailed for the first time from Southampton, bound for the United States with nearly 15,000 troops on board.

From then on the repatriation programme was in full swing, with most of the famous liners taking part, as well as US warships. And when the troops had been moved, there came the 'GI Brides' on their way to a new life across the Atlantic. In all, 14th Major Port shipped – 11,817,111 tons of cargo (3,566,125 tons deadweight)
3,640,165 personnel
228,016 casualties
194,606 German prisoners of war
21,545 railway engines and trucks
250,000 vehicles.
10,915 vessels handled.

For its achievements, the unit was granted the Meritorious Service Award.

The physical remains
Although Overlord and D-Day, and even the war itself, have passed into history, inevitably there are reminders still to be found throughout our local area. In the grounds of Chamberlain Hall, the Southampton University hall of residence in Glen Ayre Road is a well preserved octagonal pill-box and there is another at the entrance to Hamble Airfield. Tank traps can be seen along the shoreline at Eastney by the ferry which runs to Hayling Island, and in the recreation ground at Upper Shirley in Southampton. These date from the grim days of 1940 and are only quoted as samples of the many traces of anti invasion defences which still exist.

The human casualties of war are generally associated with the vast cemeteries in Flanders and Northern France, but there are two official burial sites in the area. A walk through the Victoria Country Park at Netley, past the chapel which is all that is left of the military hospital and over the remains of the railway tracks which brought in many of the casualties, will lead the visitor to the military cemetery. This contains graves of servicemen and their dependants from Victorian times right through the Second World War – including headstones marking the burial places of allies from Belgium, Poland and Czechoslovakia, and one-time enemies from Germany. Another official war cemetery is located at Hollybrook Cemetery in Southampton, behind the General Hospital.

Of the D-Day period, many of the hards and slipways remain, now used by marinas and yacht building firms. The Southampton

Contented looking German prisoners in the cage on Western Esplanade, Southampton. Southampton City Museums, Hallett Jerrard Collection

Jerry cans of petrol being loaded on to barges at Southampton.

Southampton City Museums, Hallett Jerrard Collection

Colonel Kiser, commanding officer of 14th Major Port, with Mr H. Biddle, the Docks Manager. *Southampton City Museums, Hallett Jerrard Collection*

RMS Queen Mary *entering Southampton Docks in her wartime grey paint.*
Southampton City Museums, Hallett Jerrard Collection

War graves at Hollybrook Cemetery, Southampton. *A. Kemp collection*

US battleship in Southampton Docks in early 1945.
Southampton City Museums, Hallett Jerrard Collection

Loaded and waiting at Hardway, Gosport. *Ron Brown*

The plaque placed on the Mayflower Memorial in Southampton by 14th Major Port.   A. Kemp collection

1939 — 1945
THIS TABLET WAS PRESENTED TO THE SOUTHERN RAILWAY BY THE
14TH MAJOR PORT, UNITED STATES ARMY, IN PROUD AND GLORIOUS
MEMORY OF THE MEN AND WOMEN OF THE FORCES OF THE
UNITED NATIONS WHO SAILED FROM THIS PORT DURING THE GREAT
WAR AGAINST AGGRESSION TO SECURE THE FREEDOM OF MANKIND.

LEO J. MEYER COLONEL TC.   Sherman L. Kiser COLONEL TC.
DEPUTY PORT COMMANDER.   PORT COMMANDER.

Memorial plaque presented to the Southern Railway by 14th Major Port and placed on Dock Gate No. 8.

Common was cleared after the war, following a period as accommodation for displaced persons, but the wanderer in the various wooded areas in South Hampshire can still find the concrete bases of huts and vehicle standings here and there. The requisitioned buildings have long since reverted to civilian use and generally there are no reminders of the war-time function. An exception, however, was the desire of 14th Major Port to record their thanks to various bodies in Southampton. Before leaving, they presented bronze plaques which were fixed at Dock Gate 8, the entrance to the Polygon Hotel, the foyer of the Civic Centre and on the Mayflower Memorial.

The text of the latter reads –

      1944   1945

This tablet was presented by the 14th Major Port, United States Army in proud tribute to over two million men and women of the United States forces who, together with their gallant allies, sailed from Southampton between 'D' Day, June 6th, 1944, and the day of victory to liberate the continent of Europe from aggression, in order that the freedom for which the Pilgrim Fathers strove should not be lost.

Leo J. Meyer	Sherman L. Kiser
Colonel, T.C.	Colonel T.C.
Deputy Port Commander	Port Commander

ACKNOWLEDGEMENTS

For one who has previously been engaged in charting the wider story of the war in books, articles and on film, writing the local history of the Overlord period has been a personal voyage of discovery. I am most grateful to Nicholas Pine, the publisher, for asking me to undertake it and only regret that I did not have a few years to burrow more intensively in the various military archives.

The greatest service to the local historian is provided by the librarians and archivists in his or her locality. With regard to Hampshire County Council and the municipalities of Portsmouth and Southampton, we are extremely well provided for. I offer my grateful thanks to the County Library Service and the City Archivists of both Portsmouth and Southampton for their time and trouble. I am also grateful to the staff of the 'News' Portsmouth, for allowing me to pillage their cuttings library and photographic collection. My only hope is that other local people will pursue this theme and endeavour to fill in the many gaps that I have left.

Bibliography

There is no standard work on the subject and a full list of books on Overlord and the Normandy campaign would fill a tome twice as large as this! I have, however, made great use of – Bernard Knowles. *Southampton, the English Gateway*. Hutchinson, 1951.

General works
For background information, I have naturally consulted the memoirs of the main participants – Eisenhower, Churchill, Montgomery, Alanbrooke etc.

For detailed technical background of the planning and execution of Overlord, I consulted the Official History of the campaign, volume I –
L.F. Ellis. *Victory in the West*. H.M.S.O. 1962

General works which give some detail of the preparations for Overlord in Hampshire –
Butcher, Harry C. *Three Years with Eisenhower*. Heinemann. 1946
D'Este, Carlo. *Decision in Normandy*. Collins, 1983
Lovat, Lord. *March Past*. Weidenfeld & Nicolson. 1978
Ryan, Cornelius. *The Longest Day*. Various editions
Wilmot, Chester. *Struggle for Europe*. Collins, 1952

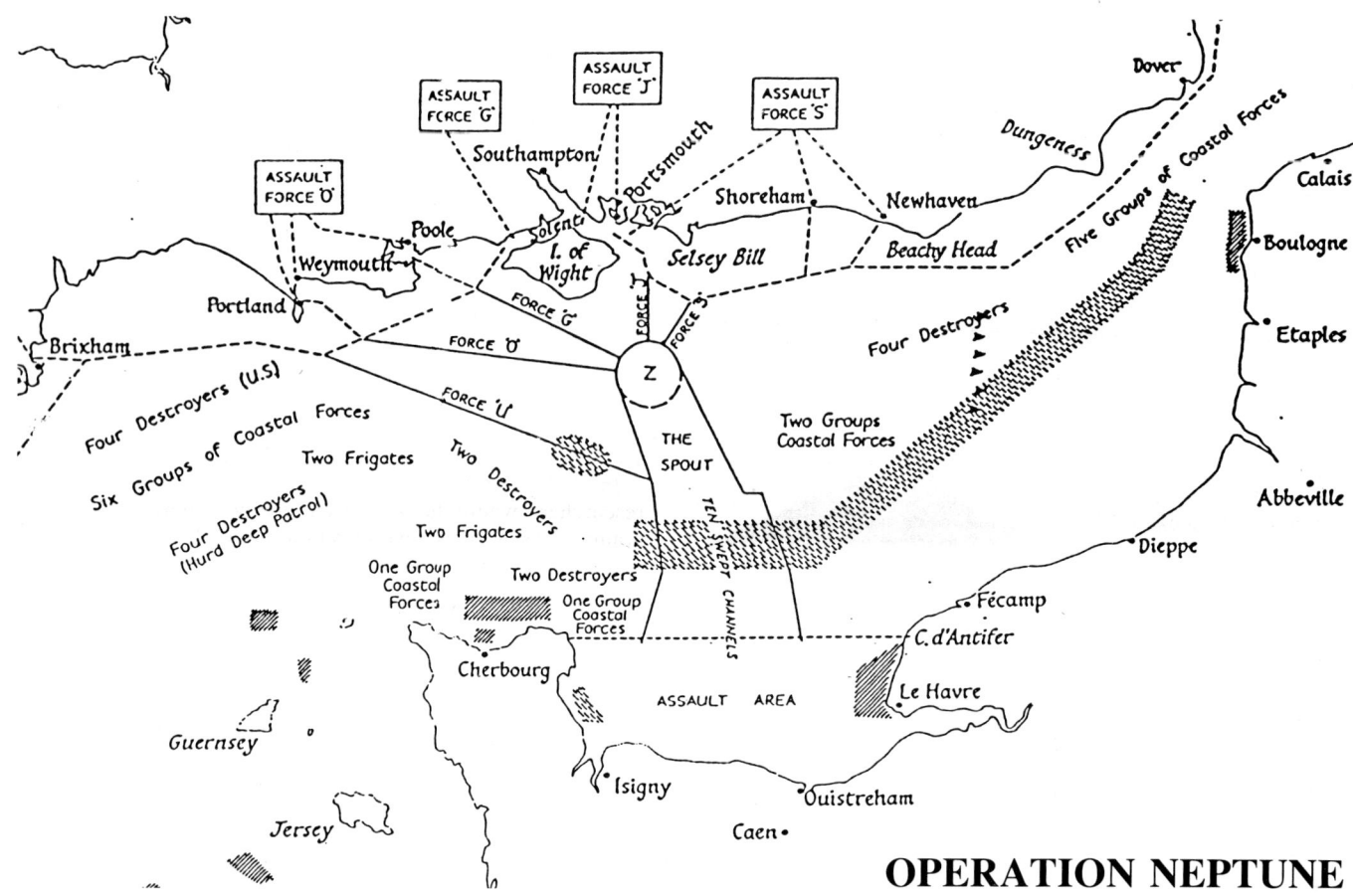

ASSAULT FORCE 'O'

ASSAULT FORCE 'G'

ASSAULT FORCE 'J'

ASSAULT FORCE 'S'

Dover

Dungeness

Five Groups of Coastal Forces

Calais

Boulogne

Southampton

Portsmouth

Shoreham

Newhaven

Etaples

Poole

Solent

I. of Wight

Selsey Bill

Beachy Head

Four Destroyers

Weymouth

FORCE 'G'

FORCE 'S'

Portland

FORCE 'O'

FORCE 'J'

Brixham

FORCE 'U'

Z

Two Groups Coastal Forces

Abbeville

Four Destroyers (U.S)

Six Groups of Coastal Forces

Two Frigates

Two Destroyers

THE SPOUT

Dieppe

Four Destroyers (Hurd Deep Patrol)

Two Frigates

TEN SWEPT CHANNELS

Fécamp

One Group Coastal Forces

Two Destroyers

C. d'Antifer

One Group Coastal Forces

Le Havre

Cherbourg

ASSAULT AREA

Guernsey

Isigny

Ouistreham

Jersey

Caen

OPERATION NEPTUNE